My Life in Northern Saskatchewan in the 1920s and 1930s

Buster Latimer
Lois Miller Latimer

Order this book online at www.trafford.com
or email orders@trafford.com

Most Trafford titles are also available at major online book retailers.

Print information available on the last page.

ISBN: 978-1-6987-0246-9 (sc)
ISBN: 978-1-6987-0244-5 (hc)
ISBN: 978-1-6987-0243-8 (e)

Library of Congress Control Number: 2020913008

Trafford rev. 07/18/2020

 www.trafford.com
North America & international
toll-free: 1 888 232 4444 (USA & Canada)
fax: 812 355 4082

To Dad, Mother, Bob, Maxine, and June

PROLOGUE

For quite some time I have wanted to share my story about life in Canada. Growing up in northern Saskatchewan during the 1920's and 1930's was a life that will never be experienced on this earth again. It was a hard life, but a good and simple life.

To begin my story, it is necessary to climb up a few branches of my family tree because my story is entwined with that of my parents and grandparents. Life is a never ending story continuing through one generation and into the next.

My parents met while my mother was working as house help for the Bridger family in South Grove, Illinois. Mabel Bridger was my dad's aunt and she introduced them. Times were hard and people moved to where they could find work. The budding relationship was interrupted when Mother moved to Anderson, Indiana. While in Anderson, she worked at a company that manufactured cardboard boxes and also helped her sister with seamstress work. In 1919, my dad followed her to Anderson so he could continue to court her. He worked at Remy Electric, a company that manufactured starters and alternators. Then on February 28, 1920, George Latimer married Bessie Tweed at the Methodist Church Parsonage. Dad did not like the work he was doing in Anderson so they moved back to Dekalb to farm.

The Latimer family has farmed for generations. According to family history, we have been farmers since the 1400s. Originally from England, the Latimer family relocated to Ireland and eventually immigrated to America in 1866. We continue to farm to this day and have farmed the Latimer farm since 1898. It became a centennial farm in 1998 and I reside there still.

Now to climb a little further up the family tree, my dad's mother, Carolyn Rich Latimer, died April 24, 1910, when Dad was only eleven. His older brother, Ray Latimer, was farming the family farm on shares with their dad, James Latimer. Upon returning to Dekalb, Dad farmed with his brother, but there was not enough work to support them all. My dad's two uncles, George and Frank Rich, were farming in Craik, Saskatchewan, and they needed help. So one month after my sister Maxine was born on February 12, 1921, Dad, Mother and Maxine moved to Craik. And this is where my story begins.

THE TWENTIES

Dad, Mother and Maxine had been living up in Craik for about a year and a half before I was due to arrive on the scene. Delivering a baby out on the frontier apparently was not something Mother was eager to experience because one month before her due date she returned to Dekalb.

I was born on September 24, 1922. We stayed in Dekalb for six months, returning in the spring of 1923. Before leaving Craik Mother negotiated the terms for our return. Dad, Mother and Maxine had been living on the farm with George and Sara Rich. When we returned Mother wanted her own home. And so, when we arrived we moved into our brand new house. When Frank Rich met me for the first time he said, "Well look, here's little Buster." And that name became my lifelong nickname.

Our new house in Craik.

The picture my mother took of me in my sailor suit.

I do not remember much of Craik. The family only lived there for three years. In 1924, my dad's friend Harvey Armstrong had bought a farm in Tisdale, which was about 200 miles north of Craik. Harvey told Dad about the farm next to his and Dad went to check it out. Dad had made good money in Craik and this was a good opportunity. So in the spring of 1925, our family moved to Tisdale. Craik was on the prairie, while Tisdale was in the bush country.

Mother, Maxine and I traveled by train and arrived two days ahead of Dad. He was also traveling by train, but he was moving the horses, the cattle and the furniture and this made for very slow travel. Arriving in Tisdale are some of my very first memories. We stayed with our friends, the Armstrongs, until Dad arrived. They had four children: George, Angus, Ivan and Adrian. Adrian was a baby, Ivan was my age, Angus was two years older and George was four years older. George and Angus had a dog that pulled a sled. On our second day in Tisdale, they took Maxine for a sleigh ride. It was all going well until the sleigh overturned and Maxine went face first into the snow. The boys brought her back into the house fussing and crying. I remember George saying to Maxine, "Wasn't it fun until you got 'felt'off?'"

Dad arrived and we moved into our new home. We had very little furniture, just a table and chairs, our beds and a clock. My parents had bought the clock in Anderson, Indiana. It traveled from Anderson to Dekalb to Craik and now to our new home in Tisdale. In the summer of 1925, Mother took a picture of me on the back porch wearing a sailor suit. I still have the picture.

Our new home in Tisdale was a small house that measured a spacious twenty feet by twenty four feet. It had a living room/dining and two bedrooms. Mother and Dad slept in one bedroom, Maxine had the other bedroom and I slept in the living room on a sofa that turned into a bed. We had a wood-burning stove in the dining room with a speckled glass door that allowed the light from the fire to show through. There was a trap door to the cellar in the living room. The cellar was not very big, maybe five feet deep. This was where we stored potatoes, carrots, radishes, parsnips and onions. There was a porch on the east side of the house that my dad enclosed for the kitchen. The kitchen was about 12 feet by 8 feet and had shelves, counter, ice box and cook stove.

The only light we had was from a kerosene lamp, which we lit in the evenings or when Mother worked in the kitchen. We had a kerosene lantern to light the way to the barn when we did the chores. We always had a good supply of matches.

Our farm was on the edge of the wilderness. It was one hundred and sixty acres with lots of trees: spruce, poplar and red willow. There were fruit trees: Saskatoon, cranberries, choke cherries, pin cherries, goose berries, black current and raspberries bushes. There were also wild strawberry patches.

Top: *A picture of me holding a snowshoe hare.* **Right:** *Maxine and I exploring the creek near our home.*

There was a lot of wildlife: deer, weasels, rabbits, beavers, coyotes, mink, and occasionally moose and bears. In the evenings, the coyotes liked to do a lot howling. They never bothered anyone. I think they were mostly afraid of us. There were Jack rabbits, which were bigger than other rabbits. They had big ears and were high speed animals and too fast for the coyote to catch. There were snowshoe hares, which were gray in the summer and turned white in the winter. The hare's back feet were large so they could run fast in the snow. They were plentiful and lived nearby in the woods and around the buildings. They climbed on the hay stacks and ate the clover leaves off the hay. Weasels were small animals with fur similar to a mink. They also turned white in the winter time. Many in the area would trap weasels and sell the hide to a furrier. Not us though, we were farmers not hunters or trappers. It was truly a land of plenty.

Our farm had a creek that ran through it. A driveway from the road ran between the house and the buildings and then out to the fields. Our house was on the east side of the drive. Behind the house was the garden. My mother always had a big garden that had a fence around it to keep out the sheep and turkeys. She grew plenty of flowers and vegetables, including carrots, radishes, celery, potatoes, peas, beans, cucumbers and parsnips.

To the west of the driveway, was the chicken house. Behind the chicken house was the barn; behind the barn was the pig pen. Also behind the barn were the haystacks and nearby three grain bins. The barn had a driveway through the center with stalls and a calf pen on one side and milk stantions and feed room on the other side. We had six milk cows, four horses, 20 sheep, 50 hens and two mother pigs.

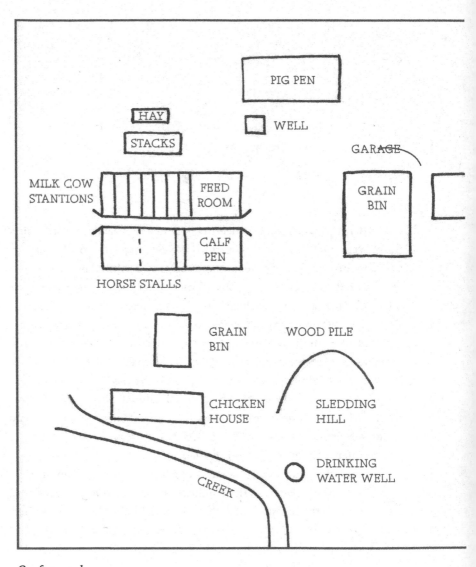

Our farm yard

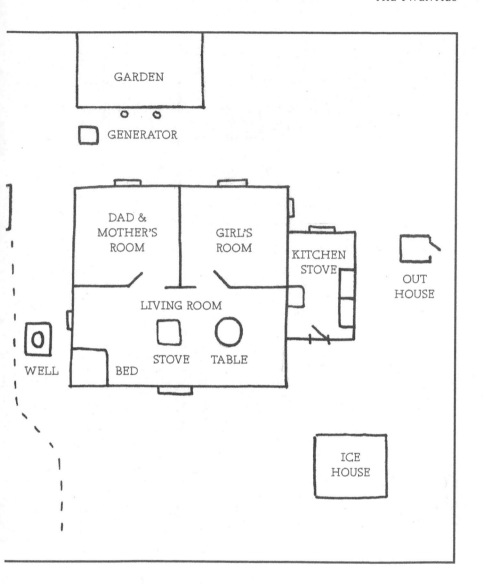

LATIMER FARM

90 ACRES FARMING
160 ACRES TOTAL

FIELD

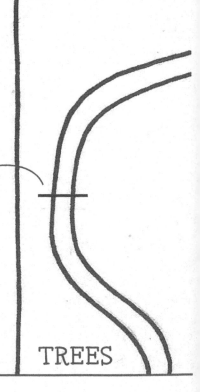

SWIMMING HOLE

TREES

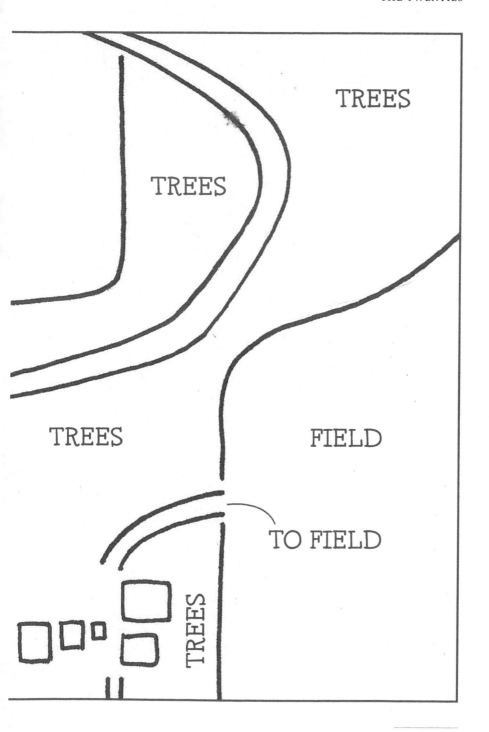

Farms in the neighboring area

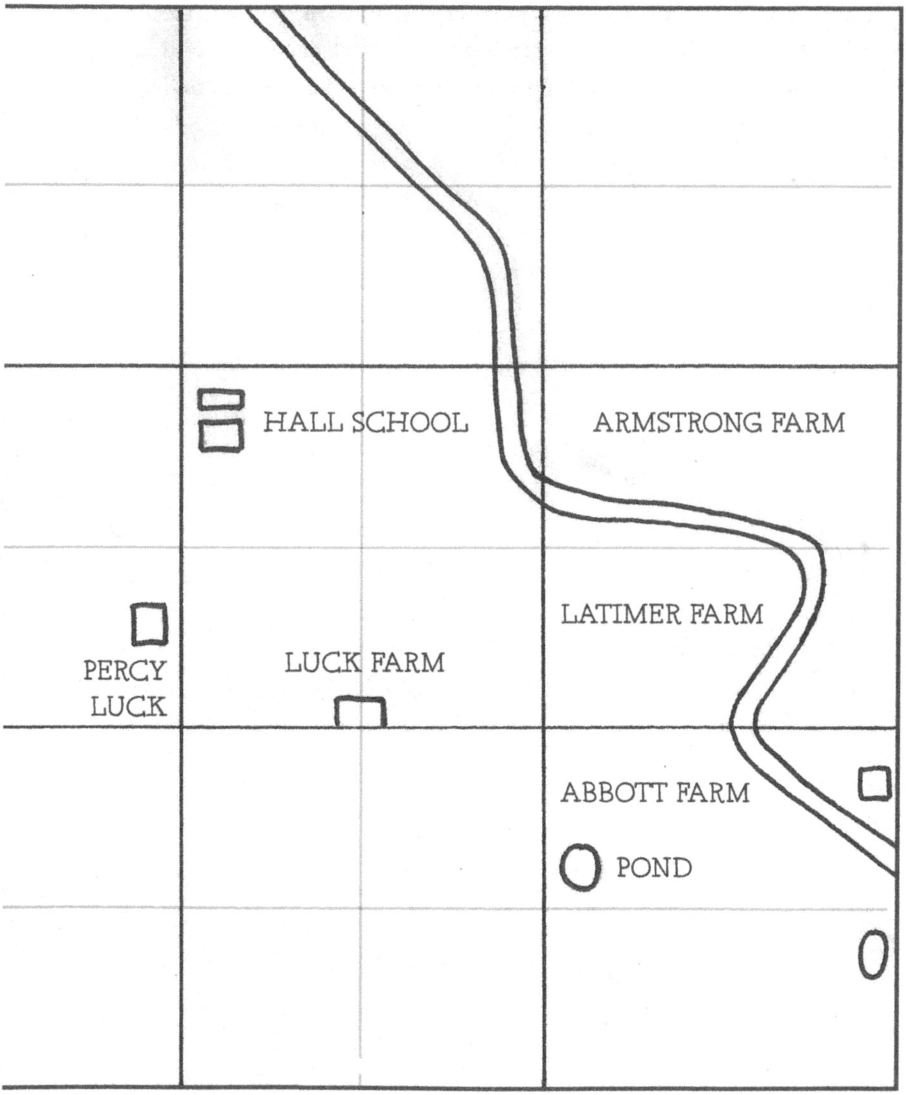

HALL SCHOOL

ARMSTRONG FARM

LATIMER FARM

PERCY
LUCK

LUCK FARM

ABBOTT FARM

O POND

Every summer Dad would clear more ground to farm. This was on-going work that continued the whole time we lived in Canada. First Dad would cut down the trees. Then with two horses he would attempt to pull out the stumps. If the stumps would not budge, Dad would cut at the roots and try again. At this point, one of our neighbors plowed the ground with a tractor and a one bottom breaking plow. After this, Dad would disc the

Threshing machines

area two or three times using a horse and small disc. He would pick up the roots and then disc it again. This new soil grew real nice wheat. Dad would eventually clear ninety acres of ground. He was the last generation to clear farm land in this way.

In the springtime when temperatures rose to above freezing, the snow melted fast and water was running everywhere. Our little creek was full but it never flooded. The snow would be gone by the middle of April. All vegetation was turning green and spring work began. Dad started planting in early May. Wheat went in first then barley and oats.

The wheat would be ready to harvest in August. I can vividly remember an August in 1926, when I was almost four years old. Uncle Ray, Dad's brother, and his friend Lee Nelson had come from Dekalb to help with the wheat harvest. Dad was cutting the wheat with a grain binder and making bundles while Ray and Lee "stooked" the bundles in rows to be threshed. In Canada, a shock of grain was called a stook. Each "stook" had ten bundles of wheat. There were 100 rows, with 20 "stooks" in each row. It was hard work on a hot summer day. I remember Uncle Ray asking me to bring him something to drink. I went to the house and returned with a jug of ginger water, a nourishing harvest drink. Although I was only three years old, this was how I helped with the harvest.

With the wheat cut and "stooked", Dad was ready for the threshing crew. Dave Luck lived on the farm to the west of us. He owned and operated the threshing machine and a 1020 John Deere tractor that powered it. Basically this is how it worked: the tractor engine turned a long belt from a pulley on the tractor to a pulley on the driveshaft of threshing machine.

There were six men on the threshing team. Three men with their team of horses would be in the field loading the "stooks" on the wagon with the cut ends out. When their wagons were full, they would pull up alongside of the threshing machine. Grabbing the cut end, each bundle was placed, grain head first, on the conveyor belt. The conveyor belt moved the bundle into the threshing machine where it separated the grain from the straw. The grain went into the wagon and the straw went onto the ground. When the wagon was full, the grain went into the bin by the barn. We had three bins one for wheat, one for barley and one for oats. Dad sold most of the wheat, but the barley and oats were used for livestock feed. When Dad took the wheat to town to sell, he withheld some to be milled into flour to be used at home. He would also bring a small bag of oats to be used for oatmeal. The straw from the harvest would be used for bedding for the animals, but the excess was burned. During harvest, the glow of haystack fires would dot the countryside for miles. It was really something to see.

Threshing took all day, from sunrise to sunset. Mother was responsible for feeding the men on the threshing team. She fed them five meals: breakfast at 7 o'clock, a morning snack at 9:30, dinner at noon which consisted of meat and potatoes, a vegetable, bread and pie, then an afternoon snack at 2 o'clock and supper at the end of the day. Margie Luck our neighbor did lend her a hand with preparing and serving the meals.

I can remember two other events that occurred that summer of 1926. First, my dad's Uncle George and Aunt Sarah Rich came to visit us from Craik. They drove the two hundred miles to Tisdale in a model T Ford. The journey took all day. It was late in the evening when they arrived. I was in bed asleep, but was awakened by the sound of talk and laughter. I got up out of bed curious about what was going on. I remember sitting on my dad's lap as they visited. They stayed for two days then returned to Craik.

The second memory was when my brother Bob was born. Bob was born at home on August 24, 1926. A midwife and a doctor had come out to the farm. My dad, Maxine and I waited in the barn until the doctor finally came out and told us we had a little brother. Later I learned that Mother had a difficult delivery, which is probably why both a midwife and doctor were there.

Winter came early in Saskatchewan. Snow would begin in early October. Days were short, cold, snowy and often windy. We never knew one day to the next what the weather would bring. We knew nothing about the wind chill, but -50 degrees with 40 mile per hour winds and drifting snow was to be expected. This was a typical winter in Canada. There was only eight hours of sunlight. The sun rose at 8:30am and set at 4pm. Many nights the northern lights danced across the sky to beat the band.

For Christmas in 1926, my dad came home with a box and told Maxine and me to open it, when we did out jumped a little puppy. He was a black and white collie. We named him Clinker. He was a good dog and our best friend and boon companion for many years. Mother, Dad, Maxine, Bob and I went to the Christmas program held in the hall next to the school.

We sang carols and watched a Christmas play. There was a Christmas tree and Santa Claus handed out small gifts and an apple.

When the temperatures reached -20, Mother thought it was warm enough to go outside to play. Maxine and I would sled down a small hill near our house that went down to the creek. Sometimes we would go out after supper and play by the light of the moon. We had a small sled and a scoop shovel. I sat on the shovel with the handle between my legs. We would slide down and climb back up over and over, all evening. We wore mittens, not gloves, because mittens kept our fingers warmer. We also wore a took. In Canada, a hat was called a took. Of course there was no radio or television. So we did what we could to pass the time during the long, dark winter evenings. Friends of Mother and Dad, Walter and Lillian Smith, would come over a couple of times a week and play Chinese checkers. After Bob was asleep, Mother and Dad, Walter and Lillian, Maxine and I would sit down and play all evening. It was a fun way to pass the time.

By this time, I was well acquainted with the neighbor kids. Our farm was centrally located with the Armstrong farm to the north and the Abbott farm to the south. We knew the Armstrongs since our coming to Tisdale, but it did not take long to get to know the Abbott family. Rodney Abbott was my age. He had five sisters and three brothers: Margaret, Dorothy, Frances, Myrtle, Ruth, Murray, Eric and Fred. We were quite the gang and rough play was inevitable when we all gathered together to sled down our hill.

Sometime in mid-winter, Dad would cut ice to fill our ice house. The ice house was located southeast of the house and the ice he cut would last the entire year. The lake where Dad cut the ice was about one mile from our house. When the ice was 16 inches thick Dad and three other men would work together to cut the ice. It took three to four days to complete the work. One would cut the ice using an ice saw. A hole would be made in the ice and one end of the saw lowered in. Then, he sawed making two straight cuts across the ice about 20 feet long. He could not stop sawing or the saw would freeze to the ice. With an ax, someone would break the ice free and then cut it into 16 inch blocks. Someone else would lift the blocks out of the water using ice tongs and load the blocks on the sled. One full load would be fifty blocks. The ice would be placed in the ice house with two inches of sawdust between each block to keep it from melting. One hundred blocks fit nicely into our ice house. We used the ice to keep food cold in the summer. We had an icebox in the kitchen and a well west of the house where we stored meat, milk and other dairy products. This was our means of refrigeration.

Something happened to me in August of 1927 that I am reminded of every day. My mother kept her washing machine in the ice house next to the house. The ice house was a nice cool place to play in the summertime. The washing machine operated by moving a handle back and forth. This back and forth movement rotated gears that turned the wash tub and the agitator in the center of the tub. I was moving the handle as fast as I could. The gears were turning and the tub was spinning faster and faster. It was great fun and I wanted to slow it down and do it again. So, I put my right hand up to the gears to stop it. It seemed like a good idea at the time, but it ended up crushing the fourth finger on my right hand.

The commotion that followed brought Mother out of the house and Dad from the fields. Mother wrapped my hand in a towel while Dad hitched the horses to the buggy. Mother rushed me to the doctor in Tisdale seven miles away. The tip of finger could not be saved and was amputated at the first joint. I am sure some kind of anesthetic was used but I cannot remember anything specifically. I had to wear a bandage for a long time. Mother made a cover like a finger from a glove that I would tie around my wrist. To this day, my finger aches at times and seems to get colder quicker than the others.

That fall, shortly after the washing machine incident, I started school. I was eager to go. Maxine had started the year before. The Armstrongs and the Abbotts went so naturally I wanted to go too. Our school was called Salopian School. It was a two-and-a-half-mile walk that took about 30 minutes. Often, as we walked to school, we would see deer along the road. Classes began at 9am and dismissed at 3pm. The school was a large building with a bell tower, three rooms and a front and rear entrance. Most of the kids used the rear entrance because this was where the large wood burning stove was. From this room, there were two doors to the classroom. In the classroom, the south wall was all windows. The school taught grades one through eight. There were five students in grade one, including me. In the entire school, there were about 30 students. My teacher's name was

Salopian School

Miss Leaukes. She was my teacher for grades one through three. She was in her late twenties I would guess. She was a good teacher and very nice. She lived with the Luck family who lived down the road from us. The schoolyard was large with a baseball field and soccer field, swings and teeter totter. There was a flag pole in front of the school that displayed the Union Jack, the flag of Britain, because Canada was under British rule. Every morning one of the older boys would come early to raise the flag and start the fire in the stove.

On my first day of school I met many new kids. They were all curious about my finger and why I was wearing a bandage. I shared the whole story doing my best to deliver a thrilling tale knowing that first impressions often leave lasting impressions. While at school, I worked hard at my studies but I also had a lot of fun. At recess, I played baseball or soccer. During class, the boys played a secret game of stealth and cunning. With a hollow reed that grew along the road and a choke cherry pit, they would pelt each other in the back of the head when the teacher was not looking. Pits were flying every which way. One time a pit whizzed right by the teacher's head just missing her and bounced off the blackboard. Sadly, that brought the game to an abrupt end. Aside from learning reading, writing and arithmetic, I learned from the other boys how to make a whistle from a poplar sprig. It needed to be a hollow Nichol Poplar sprig about five inches long and as big as my little finger. First, I cut one end at a 45 degree angle for the mouth piece. Next, I cut a notch 90 degrees on top of the whistle for air flow. Then, I carefully stripped away the bark in one piece from the mouth piece end. Lastly, I cut off the mouth piece just before the notch, insert it back into the bark. Finished!

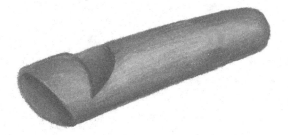

By October, the threshing would be done and the snow would begin. At this time, Dad would begin cutting wood. It would take about three weeks to cut enough wood to last the entire year. A fire burned in the house night and day during the winter. My dad cut the wood two miles east of our farm on land still owned by the government. It was a marsh land with lots of brush and trees. Dad cut white poplars for fire wood. These trees grew six to eight inches in diameter and 20 feet tall. First Dad would saw the tree off at the base and cut off the branches. Then he would load 35 to 40 logs onto the sleigh and then haul it to our yard. Dad would haul 25 loads each fall. When this was done Roy Abbott came by with his buzz saw. Roy would travel from farm to farm sawing wood. Dad had him cut the logs into 16 inch lengths, which would fit nicely into our stove. After the logs were cut, our neighbors Percy and Dave Luck would help Dad split the wood into quarters. This took about a day. The wood would then be neatly stacked in a pile south of the barn between the barn and the road. Let winter come, we were ready.

There was a saw mill across the road from our farm that was owned by the Abbott family. The mill operated all winter up until spring field work began. This was how the operation ran. A person would drop off a load of logs and place an order for whatever size lumber he needed: 1x4, 1x6, 2x4, 2x6, 2x12 or whatever. The orders were lined up and completed one at a time. When the order was done, the person returned to pick up his lumber.

One day, when I was about five years old, I went across the road to watch. Ernie Abbott came over to me and said I was welcome to watch if I

Abbott saw mill

stayed safely out of the way. He showed me where to stand where I would not be their way. A big tractor powered the saw in the same way as a threshing machine. Six men ran the operation. One man with a horse would haul a log from the pile to the saw. Ernie Abbott and another man would lift and roll the log onto the saw table. Arthur Abbott operated the table. First, the log would go through the saw. Then Arthur would reverse the saw, turn the log and send it through again. He did this two more times until the bark was cut off all four sides. The slab of wood would then be cut to size and Ernie Abbott would stack the finished lumber. Fred Abbott's job was to empty sawdust out of the pit. The saw dust would be used in the ice houses throughout the area. This was no Menards and every time I browse the lumber isle I am reminded of it.

It was also about this time in 1928 that I got my first pair of ice skates. Charlie Luck, an older neighbor boy, had some skates that he had outgrown and he gave them to me. There was a pond about three quarters of a mile from our house on the Abbott farm. That winter the ice on the pond was real smooth and it stayed clear of snow most of the winter. I skated almost every day, trying hard to keep up with the older Abbott boys as they played hockey.

Eventually the temperature began to rise, the snow began to melt and the days began to grow longer. This meant that spring was on its way. One spring day, the morning temperatures were frigid, but by noon it was a pleasant 70 degrees, much too warm to be wearing long underwear and winter clothing. Adrian Armstrong was the youngest in the family and had just started school that year. During recess, he went into the stable and took off his long underwear. In a rush, his underwear was hopelessly twisted, inside out and wadded up. He played hard during recess and did not have the time or patience to untangle the mess and left it for the teacher to do. There was no limit to the work the teacher did.

Warmer temperatures also meant the end of the school year was near. This we eagerly waited for. At the end of the school year, the four schools in the area would hold a "Field Day". It would take place in Elderly, a small town six miles east of Tisdale. The events included track and field and coed softball. The event started at nine in the morning and lasted until six in the evening. The parents came to watch and they brought food for a picnic. Our school, Salopian School, placed first in both track and field and softball pretty much every year. We were a force to be reckoned with. At the end of the year, there would be a program displaying school projects and followed by the eighth grade graduation. Then, as the finale to the school year, we watched a Charlie Chaplin movie in the town hall next to the school. It was a good way to end the school year and usher in summer.

In Saskatchewan, the days are long with nineteen hours of sunlight and lots of fun. Dad and I damned up the creek west of our house to create a swimming hole. We spent many hours a day swimming there. Summer was a time for berry picking. There was a large patch of raspberry bushes on the north side of our farm. Raspberries were in season for about three weeks and we picked every three days or so while the berries lasted. It was mostly Maxine's job to pick the berries, but I helped her once. We used three quart lard pails. When Maxine's pail was full mine was only half. I confess I ate more than I put in my pail. We had Saskatoon bushes near the house. The bushes grew six to eight feet tall. We picked Saskatoon berries all summer long. We ate them fresh or on ice cream or with cream, but our favorite way of eating Saskatoon berries were baked in a pie. Everyone loved Saskatoon pie! My two favorite foods while in Canada were Saskatoon berries and honey. Honey in Canada tasted different than the honey here in Illinois because it came from the nectar of sweet clover and canola blossoms. We did not have our own bee hives but bought from our neighbor, Harold MacArthur. We always had a good supply of honey.

One nice summer day, several kids came over to play baseball. There were eight or nine kids. We divided up. Maxine was on one team and I was on the other. There was a new kid who had recently moved to the area. His name was Harry. He was just a little guy and it was the first time he had ever played baseball so he required a lot of coaching. He was on Maxine's team and somehow he managed to get to third. Third base was near the road. Someone on Maxine's team hit the ball to the outfield. Harry just stood there on third base. Maxine started hollering at him, "Run home, Harry! Run home." New to the game of baseball, Harry did as he was told. He ran down the road, over the bridge and home.

Summertime was a time to gather with friends, for socializing and picnicking. Every Sunday our neighbors would meet at the school for a potluck. The men and older boys would play baseball, the younger kids ran races and the women would sit and visit. There were five families around Tisdale that had come from the United States. Every July 4th we gathered for the Yankee picnic. These families were the Latimers, the Popes, the Machetchys, The Lee Walsh and Tom Walsh families. We would gather at one of their homes and celebrate Independence Day just like the folks back in the States.

In the summertime, Bob and I had the pleasure of sleeping outside in an empty grain bin. Normally we slept on the sofa-bed in the living room, but in the summer we would drag a mattress out to the grain bin and sleep there from May to September. It was a great adventure that lasted until harvest time. When the bin was needed to store grain we had to move back inside.

In early summer, a tribe of Indians would go past our house traveling west. They would stop at the creek and water their horses. Their horses were a paint, either black and white or brown and white. Mother would sell them bread and milk. There were about 20 of them. There were two pairs of horses, pulling two wagons. The men drove the horses and the women, holding their babies, rode in the back of the wagon sitting on the floor. Young boys rode horses bare back. The girls either walked alongside the wagon or rode with the women. They would return in the fall and again pass by our house.

Our neighbor Ernie Abbott once told us about an Indian chief who died. He and Percy and Dave Luck helped the Indians bury him. He was buried sitting up in his grave. The grave was on the side of the road west of our farm. There was a mound of dirt about three feet high off the side of the road. True story!

My sister June was born August 11, 1928. This time Mother went to Tisdale and stayed in a midwife's maternity home. She went to the home a few days before June was born. We had no phone of course, very few people did. The school, Dave Luck and Tom Walsh were the only ones who had a phone. So Dad went every day to check on Mother. Finally after one of his visits he returned home and told us we had a new sister. Mother stayed at the maternity home for about a week. She worked very hard at home and on the farm. I have often thought her stay at the home must have felt like a vacation. While she was away, Marjorie Luck looked after us at home.

THE THIRTIES

The thirties brought a lot of changes to our lives. Again in 1930 Mother took another vacation at the maternity home. My brother Bruce was born March 5, 1930. Mother and Dad were busy taking care of five children and running the farm. Now Maxine and I had to help more at home and with the chores. We had horses, cows sheep, pigs, chickens and turkeys to take care of. Twice a day, I had to take the cows and horses to the creek for water. In the winter, I had to break the ice so they could drink.

When I was eight years old, Dad taught me how to milk the cows. I sat on a three-legged stool with the pail on the floor between my knees. After milking, I took the milk to the house and poured into the separator to separate the milk from the cream. It was a big job to clean the separator afterward, but that job fell to Maxine. Later, we put the cream into the churn to make butter. The churn was a tall wooden pail that held five gallons. The lid had a hole in the center for the paddle. The paddle was at the end of a stick that came up through the hole in the lid. We took turns working the paddle up and down until the cream turned to butter which took about 20 to 30 minutes.

In the summer of 1931, Dad was clearing more land and Maxine and I were picking up the roots and brush from the newly broken ground. Early in the thirties, Dad bought a Fordson tractor and was plowing the new ground with a one bottom breaking plow. As he was doing this, he plowed up two small evergreen trees. He told me to bring my little wagon to the field and take the trees and plant them somewhere near the house. I took them and planted them next to Mother's garden gate. The trees grew very tall and were there long after we, and the garden gate, were gone.

Now that I was older, I helped Dad with more of the fieldwork. Dad grew sweet clover on what was last year's wheat ground. The hay that was raised would feed the livestock during the upcoming winter. Dad would cut the hay with a binder that made a windrow. I would be up on the hayrack and dad would pitch the hay up to me using a pitchfork. I piled it on the hayrack until it was eight feet tall. Then we took it and piled it beside the barn. After 10 to 12 loads, the haystacks stood about 14 feet tall. There would be enough hay to last all winter.

Dad was a very good and patient horseman. He had bought a gray colt from our neighbor Mr. Machetchy. We named her Fay. In the spring of 1930, Dad took me to Tisdale to buy a young horse to make a team with Fay. They had a pen of broncos. We picked out another gray horse and named him Jerry. We drove our horses, Tony and Pearl, to town that day and tied Jerry to them to lead him home. He trotted along nicely, but when we got home Dad could not get him to go inside of the barn. He had never been inside of a barn before. Boy was he a bad actor, but Dad got by. It took all summer to break him, but by fall he and Fay made a great team.

Another horse my Dad bought from Walter Smith was a nice sandy colored horse we named Sandy. Sandy had a temperamental disposition. If she did not want to move she would balk, then stand and paw the ground. She was not going anywhere until she was plenty good and ready. Walter did not have the patience for this but knew that Dad did. So Dad took her.

Once Dad and Maxine where going to town on a nice winter day to get some groceries. Dad harnessed Sandy and hitched her up to the cutter. A cutter is a sleigh on two high runners. It had a cushion seat and there was only room for two. Dad pulled up to the house and Maxine got into the cutter. Dad shook the reins and said, "Giddy up," and Sandy put on the old stall act. She started pawing the snow with her front hoof. Dad knew they were not going anywhere. He unhitched Sandy and took her back to the barn. Half an hour later he went back to the barn. This time Maxine was in the sleigh waiting while dad hitched her up. Then Dad jumped in the cutter, shook the reins, said, "Giddy up," and Sandy took off for town in a nice little trot. They got to town and tied Sandy to the hitching rail at the stable. When they had finished their errands and were heading for home, Sandy decided to pull the old stall act just outside of town. Dad got out of the cutter and took Sandy by the halter and turned her back towards town. Dad got back in the cutter and Sandy took off for town. Dad drove her through town and around the block. After doing that Sandy was ready to go and headed for home in a nice little trot.

We had another horse named Barney. Barney was a nice, gentle horse and in the winter pulled us to school on our toboggan. I would be in front driving then Maxine, Bob and June would line up behind. One day before school, Dad and I were milking the cows and Bob took Barney to the creek to give him water. Bob got fooling around doing something and paying no attention to the task at hand. In the meantime, Barney took himself home and finding the barn door closed, he took himself off to school. We had no toboggan ride that day. We walked and when we got to school there was Barney waiting in his stall.

In 1932, life changed for us in a big way. That summer Dad bought a Model T Ford. This meant we could travel further and be much more mobile. It had a front and back seat. Dad, Bob and I sat up front. Mother, with Bruce on her lap, June and Maxine all sat in back. The car had a canvas top and curtains that snapped on in case it rained. Now that we had a car we went to town every Saturday night. Every Saturday night as we were driving to town, an old bachelor neighbor named Gordon Jones would be standing by the side of the road waiting for someone to give him a ride to town. We would stop. "Go'in ta town, Ay?" he asked. Our car was already full, but Bob and I would slide over and crowd in to make room for him up front. Gordon lived next to the school and donated the land to build the school. He gave the school its name, Salopian School. We expected to see Gordon waiting at the corner east of the school every Saturday night. One time, we were driving along and a mile up the road Gordon yelled to Dad, "Stop, stop, George! That's a blame skunk." Dad got the car stopped and missed the skunk. Crisis averted!

We went to town to socialize, but also to do errands. Mother would sell butter, eggs, cream and milk and then shop for groceries and things we might need. Bob and I would meet up with other kids and play in the streets and alleys.

One Saturday night, Bob and I were with Ivan Armstrong and Melvin and Harold Brain. They did not look for trouble, but it always seemed to find them. When we were with them, I noticed the town police always seemed to keep an eye on us. I do not know why we never did anything too awfully wrong. Every Saturday night was the same; Officer Tom Sparrow was on the alert. That evening Donald Oliphant was on the wrong end of one of Ivan's pranks. Ivan put a firecracker inside a cigarette and gave it to Donald which he gladly accepted. You can guess what happened. When it exploded, his glasses went flying off, he fell to the ground. It was so funny, but not so funny to him. He was not hurt so no harm done. This might be why the police kept an eye on us.

About twice a year, we would go to the movies. This was a real treat. We would go to the Falcon Theater, pay our 15 cents and watch Shirley Temple. Maxine loved Shirley Temple. Another time we watched "State Fair."

Now that we had a car, we could go to the fair in Tisdale. The fair held a baseball tournament every year. One of the best teams that played were the Crooked River Lumber Jacks. At fair time, the Indians set up their tents at the edge of the fair and sold clothing and leather goods. The Indians always held a horse race. There were usually about ten riders. They would start the race by firing a gun. When the gun went off the horses scattered every which way. Several riders would fall off their horses. If they were lucky, maybe two would finish the race. We never wanted to miss watching the horse race because it was the funniest thing to see. There was a bigger fair in Melfort, which was twenty five miles west of Tisdale. Now that we had a car we went to that fair too. Dad gave each of us 25 cents to spend. This was a real treat. We could buy a double dip ice cream cone for a nickel, watch one of the carnival shows for a dime and have money left over for cotton candy. On the way home from Melfort, it began to rain. We had to stop and snap on the side curtain to stay dry. The road became very muddy and we had to inch along slowly. When we finally made it home, it was well after dark.

In late summer, we would all pile into the car and go berry picking. We had raspberries and Saskatoon berries at home, but 10 miles east of our farm there was a wooded area where we picked blueberries and moss cranberries. Moss cranberries grew in shaded, mossy areas; this is why they are called moss cranberries. After picking, the berries mother would make pies and jams.

We always had plenty to eat. Mother's large garden provided fresh vegetables in the summer and enough canned vegetables to last all winter. Mother baked fresh bread every day, two loaves. Fresh bread with butter, homemade jam or honey was as good as manna from heaven. For meat, we had pork and beef. We were part of a beef ring with six other families. How this worked was every 10 weeks someone would butcher a steer and the meat would be divided between the six families. This included roasts and steaks that we stored in the well west of the house. One time, our neighbors, the Abbotts, discovered a bear hibernating in early winter. They dug him out and shot the bear. They butchered him, but the meat was terrible, tough and fatty. We also had a mother pig. Each spring she would have a litter of piglets, usually about eight. Dad would sell them but would reserve one for us. When the pig grew to 200 pounds dad butchered it and Mother would can the meat.

One fall, after a night of heavy rain, Dad went out to do the chores. He went to feed the two pigs in the pig shed north of the barn. When he got there, the pigs were gone. The gate was closed. There were no holes in the fence. All was secure. They weighed close to 200 pounds and could not have gotten out on their own. Dad trusted our neighbors, but it had to be someone who knew where the pen was and that the pigs were there. It was a real "who-done-it." I remember Dad saying, "Whoever did it must have gotten really wet." That year we had no canned meat.

Halloween in Canada was different than in the United States. It was all tricks and no treats. The tricks were done to the school house. One year I was with Ivan and Angus Armstrong and Rodney and Fred Abbott. We moved the outhouse at the school about four feet with the idea that someone walking along that Halloween night would fall in the hole. There was some retribution for the prank. My feet were frost bitten. When I walked across the wood floor it sounded like ice cubes clinking.

In the winter of 1932, I was on the school hockey team. We had a game five miles to the south at Goldburn School. It was a nice Sunday in winter. Our parents drove us to the game. Goldburn had an open air rink, down in a valley out of the wind. I remember the game. We lost, but I scored my first goal! We played Goldburn every winter but the rest of our games were in Tisdale. Most towns in Canada had a regulation sized rink with natural ice. Natural ice would freeze in October and last until March. Artificial ice was not used until late in the 1940's. The rink in Tisdale was enclosed and it was cold inside. I think sometimes it was colder inside the than it was outside. The town works took care of the rink. They had a device that re-surfaced the ice every morning to keep it nice and smooth as glass. I played hockey at the rink in Tisdale every winter up until I left in 1939.

Hockey has a long history dating back centuries, but hockey as we know it today originated in Canada. The first game was in Montréal in 1875. In the 1930's and 1940's most NHL players were from Canada. All whom, I imagine, started skating on small ponds like I did. My friends and I really admired these Canadian skaters and aspired to be like them. No different from kids today. Saskatchewan had its share of players who went to the NHL. Doug and Max Bentley were brothers from Delisle, a small town southwest of Tisdale. They played for the Chicago Blackhawks in the thir-ties and forties. Bill and Bun Cook and Lynn Patrick played for the New York Rangers. Gordy Howe was from Floral just south of Saskatoon. He had a natural instinct; skating around the ice he was always in the right place at the right time. Bobby Hull was from Ontario and played for the Black-hawks. He was the first player to use the slap shot. It was much like a golf swing that propelled the puck at a high rate of speed. After this, players started wearing helmets in the NHL. There was a difference in how the eastern Canadians and western Canadians played hockey. Hockey play-ers from the east were finesse players, hockey players from the west were all brawn.

On February 10, 1933, tragedy struck our quiet community. In the early morning hours, a disastrous fire broke out at the Imperial Hotel in Tisdale. Eight lives were lost including the proprietress, her three daugh-ters and the hotel manager. The fire started in the wood box by the stove in the Rex Café located within the hotel. The alarm was sounded, but with-in 15 minutes the hotel was a blazing inferno. Due to strong winds and a frigid -45 degree temperature they had difficulties starting the pump en-gine. The fire made rapid headway before the first streaks of water reached it. Mrs. Couture, the proprietress of the hotel, made an attempt to escape. Noticing their mother's absence the three daughters returned to assist her. Tragically all four perished in the fire. Sandy McPherson, the hotel man-ager, attempted to rescue the guests, but his efforts were fruitless. Along with being badly burned he ran bare foot leaving footprints of blood along the sidewalk, the skin being torn from his feet by the intense frost. He too died a few days later from his injuries. Dad said those bloody foot prints remained until the snow and ice melted a sad reminder of the tragic event.

Christmas in the 1930's held the same traditions. These traditions were still special just different being older. We went to the town hall for the Christmas concert. The events also included a dance. Gordon Jones, our Saturday night ride-share, never missed an event. At the dance, he would pester all the girls to dance with him. He danced around jumping like a jack rabbit. The girls hated to see him come toward them to ask for a dance. They would all dance with him and by the end of the evening he had danced with every girl. Gordon was from Wales and very likeable. He was fun to be around. Gordon was a good friend of Amos Jackson. Amos told Gordon he could marry his oldest daughter, Winny, but Winny was having nothing to do with this!

For Christmas, in 1934, we were invited to have dinner with our neighbors the Lucks. They had a new radio and were the first we knew to own one. This was really something spectacular! While everyone was listening to a radio program, Dad sent Bob and me home to do the chores. We ran home about three quarters of a mile. We fed and watered the animals then milked the six cows. It took us over an hour, but when we got back dinner was ready. After dinner, we listened to a hockey game between the Toronto Maple Leave and the Montréal Canadians.

In 1936, we would get our own radio, a gift from Aunt Julie, Mother's sister. For us to have our own radio was like having a million bucks before taxes. We spent hours listening. Mother loved the National Barn Dance on WLS in Chicago. My favorite programs were Amos and Andy, Edgar Burgan and Fibber McGee and Molly. We had great reception from stations in both the United States and Canada: WHO from Des Moines, KOA Denver, KSL in Salt Lake City. We had no electricity. To power the radio Dad built a 16 foot windmill behind the house. He attached a car alternator to the windmill blade, from the alternator a wire ran into the house and attached to the radio battery.

One time, our friends Ernie and Rodney Abbott came over to listen to the heavyweight boxing match between Joe Lewis and Max Schmeling.

It was the fight of the century and Ernie did not want to miss it. He even brought his own battery as a backup just in case. Dad was tuning in the radio and just as it was coming in clearly they heard the announcer counting. We could not believe it. Joe Lewis had knocked out Max Schmeling in the first round! It was the quickest fight in history lasting two minutes and four seconds.

Now what to do with the afternoon? Maxine, Bob, June, Bruce and I decided to go sledding. We usually went sledding on the hill in front of our house. This time I thought we should try a larger, steeper hill west of the barn. I thought it would be fun to try this instead. The only problem was it had a few trees in the way. We looked it over. Still not sure if this was a good idea we decided to send Bruce on the maiden voyage. He almost made it to the bottom before plowing into a tree. After that, we decided it would be best to go back to our old hill.

In the middle 1930's, winter travel changed. Vans were replacing horse-drawn cutters and sleighs. A van was enclosed and was about six feet wide, six feet high and eight feet long. There were two doors on each side and windows in front and on the sides. There was a small wood burning stove in the front corner with a four inch chimney through the roof that kept the van nice and warm. It had two runners and was pulled by two horses. Ernie Abbott was the first one to build a van. Soon everyone was building

A neighbor's van

vans, including Dad. The roads were never plowed and vans made winter travel much more comfortable.

In 1936, it was now my turn, as one of the older boys, to go to school early and help with the chores. I would raise the flag and get ice out of the ice house, rinse off the saw dust then chop it up for drinking water. In the winter, I started the fire in the wood burning stove so that the school house had plenty of time to warm up before the younger children arrived. That spring I received my 8th grade diploma. Some of the girls would continue their education by going to high school in Tisdale. Those who did usually stayed with family in town. As for Maxine and me, we stayed on at Salopian School continuing our education by taking correspondence courses provided by the government. At the end of the school year, we had our Field Day event with neighboring schools. Again our school was champion of these events. Summertime brought the return of the Sunday afternoon potlucks and this year I was asked to play softball with the men.

There were a chain of events that occurred in 1937 that would change the course of my family's future. In September, Uncle Jack and Aunt Clara, Mother's brother and sister, paid us a visit. Uncle Jack had been to the Pendleton Roundup in Oregon. He was there to perform his fancy roping tricks. He performed for us too. We had never seen anything like it before. Uncle Jack would spin the rope in a large circle over his head then lower it and jump through it. It was something to see! The next morning he took us to school and put on a show for our friends. It was a big thrill for them. I saw some of them years later and they were still be talking about Uncle Jack and his roping act.

While Uncle Jack and Aunt Clara were visiting, they became very concerned about Mother's health. She worked very hard and she looked thin, tired and worn out. They encouraged her to return to the States to rest and regain her health. Eventually she did go home for three months, in the fall of 1938. The last time she was home was when I was born in 1922. She had not seen her mother or family in sixteen years. She returned to Tisdale in November with Uncle Jack and Aunt Clara. Uncle Jack had bought a ranch near Rochelle, Illinois and asked if Maxine and I would like to move to Illinois? I would help on the ranch and Maxine would help with Grandma Tweed and the housework. We also learned that Ray Latimer was looking for someone to farm the Latimer farm in Dekalb. He asked Mother if Dad would consider returning to the States. It did appear that our time in Canada was coming to an end.

That same year Bob got sick. In the fall, when he was ten years old, his legs began to ache. His legs hurt so bad that Dad would rub them in the middle of the night so he could sleep. The doctors did not know what was causing it. Eventually Bob was diagnosed with polio. It caused a deformity of his feet. He could not stand flat footed. He could only stand on the tips of his toes. His feet were only about six inches long and his toes curled under. This was another good reason to return to the States so Bob could get the care he needed.

Our last year in Canada was no different than other years. We spent our time working very hard. In the spring, I helped Dad sheer sheep. We had 15 Black Suffolk sheep. I would round them up and hold them while Dad sheered them. Then we would bundle up the fleece and took it to town to sell. The crops were planted and harvested, the hay was cut, the firewood chopped and the ice house was filled. All the usual necessary work still had to be done. In addition to this, there was a shortage of livestock feed in southern Saskatchewan. The government had asked to buy straw from farmers in our area. Dad had oat straw to sell. So he and our neighbors, Bill Williams and Walter Smith, hired a baling crew to bale up the straw. There were six men on the crew. Mother and Maxine prepared and served three meals for the men. They had a bunk house that they moved from site to site. In one day, they baled 650 bales of straw. The next day dad, Bill and Walter loaded three hayracks with 72 bales of hay. They delivered 15 loads of straw to the train in Tisdale to be shipped south. Years later, I learned that Dad was never paid.

Dad also rented and worked the Bill Brooks farm. I helped after school and on weekends. Bill Brooks loved baseball. He talked baseball to whoever would listen. On June 11, 1938, Dad and I were planting spring wheat. I remember Bill Brooks telling me about the Cincinnati Red's Johnny Vander Meer's no-hitter against the Boston Bees. Despite being a wild pitcher no Boston player made it past first base. Then four days later Vander Meer threw a second no hitter in Brooklyn. That season Johnny Vander Meer threw 21.2 consecutive innings without giving up a hit.

In the fall of 1938, I had my first real job working on the Luck threshing team. Dad and I would get up at 5am and be ready to work at 6am. I had a team of horses and a wagon. I loaded my own loads and hauled bundles of grain from the fields to the threshing machine and pitched them in. Dad and two other men loaded their own loads. We worked until 10pm. We ate breakfast at home. The farm where we were working fed us lunch at 9am, dinner at noon, lunch again at 4:30pm and supper at 10pm, quitting time. My pay was $1.00 a day. When harvest ended in early September, I returned to school and continued my correspondence courses.

In March of 1939, I played my last hockey game at the arena in Tisdale. I completed my correspondence courses and Maxine and I graduated from high school. Then on Sunday, March 15, 1939, Dad, Mother, Bob, June and Bruce took Maxine and me to the train in Tisdale where we said our good-byes. We left in the evening and would travel to Winnipeg. From Winnipeg it was a four day bus trip to Chicago. I was feeling excited. I was looking forward to my future and felt that moving to the United States would hold better opportunities for all of us. We crossed the Canadian border on St. Patrick's Day, traveled on to Fargo, North Dakota, reaching Chicago on Friday, March 20. Aunt Julie met us at the train. We spent Friday night and Saturday in Chicago with Aunt Julie and Uncle Harry. We went past Wrigley Field. She said, "That's where Gabby Hartnett hit a home run in the late innings that put the Cubs into the World Series." On Sunday, Aunt Julie and Uncle Harry drove us to the ranch in Rochelle. On the way we stopped in Oregon, Illinois, to watch "Gone with the Wind."

I worked on the ranch with Uncle Sandy, another one of Mother's brothers. Jack worked for Standard Oil Company. He was captain of an oil tanker that transported gasoline across the Atlantic to England. He would be gone for long periods of time. While he was gone, Uncle Chris, Mother's oldest brother, would manage the farm in Jack's absence. There was a family from Kentucky who also helped on the ranch. Their name was Griffin, Harold, his wife and teenage son. Harold played the guitar and sang country music. We raised corn, put up hay and took care of the cow-calf herd.

Dad, Mother, Bob, June and Bruce moved back to Dekalb in November of 1939. We were all together to celebrate our first Thanksgiving in the United States. They lived with Uncle Chris until spring when they moved to the Latimer farm on Rich Road.

Standing in front of our house on the day I left for the United States.

EPILOGUE

I worked on Uncle Jack's ranch until 1943. Uncle Jack had returned from England and was at the ranch for September and October in 1939. This would be the last time I saw him. He returned to his ship in November and was torpedoed in the north Atlantic at the beginning of World War II. He was lost at sea. This brought about much change and uncertainty. Grandma Tweed went to live with Aunt Julie in Riverside and Maxine moved back with Mother and Dad. For a time, Aunt Emma and Uncle Harry, Mother's youngest brother, took over the ranch, but eventually it was sold in 1943. After the ranch sold, I moved to Dekalb and lived with my folks.

As well as working on the ranch, I did various other jobs. In the fall of 1940, I helped our neighbors the Beardons finish picking their corn. Lee Beardon had an attack of appendicitis and needed surgery. His father, Frank, hired me to run the tractor and finish picking 40 acres of corn. When I was done, Frank paid me a good wage and told me if I ever needed work I could come and work for him anytime. That same winter I worked as a shipping clerk at the Brody's Coat Factory in Dekalb.

My brother Gary was born on February 22, 1941. Also about that time Bob had surgery on his legs in Chicago. After his surgery, Bob was able to walk and stand flat footed. The surgery had been sponsored by the Dekalb Elks Club. After this, Dad joined the Elks Club and was a lifelong member.

I was drafted in 1944, but was exempt due to the lack of farm laborers. I worked for our neighbor Frank Schweitzer. He had cattle and hogs and 260 acres of farm land west of my folks. I worked for Frank for three years. The Schweitzers were wonderful people to work for.

In 1945 Maxine, June, Bruce and I took a trip back to Tisdale in Maxine's 1940 Willys. The first night we got as far as Denison, Iowa. The second night we made it to Deadwood, South Dakota. We saw the Badlands and the Black Hills. We had never seen anything like it before. We saw the graves of Wild Bill Hickok and Calamity Jane and explored a large cave near Sturgis. From Sturgis we went to Wyoming past Devil's Tower and north through Montana where we spent the night.

The next day, we entered Saskatchewan. Our friend Walter Smith was living in Swanson, Saskatchewan. We had car trouble just before reaching Swanson. Walter picked us up and towed the car in for repairs. We stayed with the Smiths for two days while we waited for the car to be fixed. Once on the road, it took a full day to reach Tisdale. We stayed with Marjorie (Luck) Patterson and her husband Delbert for three days. We had a great time visiting our old friends. Of course there were changes since we left. Our school, Salopian School, had closed in 1942 and the students were being bused to Tisdale. Beginning in 1940, they began using bulldozers to clear the land of trees and brush and also to plow snow from the road. These were big changes from the experiences I knew. We started for home and had car trouble again in Manitoba. We left the car and came home on the bus. Dad had to go back with the parts, repair the car and drive it home.

In 1947, Dad rented more land. So I stopped working for the Schweitzers and started farming with my dad. In 1948, I bought my first car, a 1946 Chevy. I made a lot of good friends in Dekalb. I played baseball with several clubs in the area, the Malta/Dekalb Blue Socks, Sycamore Sons and the Dekalb County Farm Bureau. I was a part of the Rural Youth organization. Rural Youth was sponsored by the Farm Bureau. They organized suppers and square dances. I took some trips out west. I was having a blast!

In 1948, Bob, Ed Lothson, Dale Herrman and I took my new car on a road trip to Texas, New Mexico, Arizona, Nevada, Utah and Wyoming. We had such a good time we did it again over the next two years visiting different states. In 1951, Ed Lothson, Walt Lambert, Jerry Walsh and I went to the Canadian Rockies, to Alberta, Calgary, Banff National Park, Lake Louise and the Columbia Icefields. Then we crossed the Continental Divide and went into British Columbia to see Glacier National Park.

Maxine got married in 1948. June was married in 1953 and moved to San Diego. Bob moved to California and worked repairing radios for Collins Electronics. Bruce went into the Army and served in Korea.

In 1951, I went to Champaign to play baseball in the Farm Bureau Sports Festival. There was also a square dance competition which I participated in as part of Rural Youth. We placed 2nd in the baseball tournament and 1st in the square dance competition.

I had just bought a new Pontiac. The girls from Rural Youth had no way of getting to Champaign so I lent them my new Pontiac. One of the girls was Charlene O'Donnell. Charlene and I started dating in 1953. On our first date, we were driving past the popcorn stand in Sycamore. Charlene said, "Doesn't that popcorn smell good!" I said, "I'll drive around the block so you can smell it again." Later it occurred to me that maybe she wanted some popcorn. As they say, hindsight is 20/20, but it must not have been too big of a blunder because not only did she go out with me again, she married me. We were married April 11, 1953, and have been married for sixty-seven years.

Many years have passed since the time we lived in Canada, but every time we would get together, talk always seemed to lead to stories about Canada. Dad, Mother, Bob, Maxine and June are now gone but I still have treasured memories that are just as vivid as the day they happened. I am two years shy of witnessing a century and I have many more stories, but I will end here. Besides, now you are part of my story and are able to tell it just as well.

Charlene and I were married on April 11, 1953 in DeKalb.

*Top: The two pine trees I planted in 1931. They were still standing fifty years later in 1981. **Bottom:** Leslie, Audrey, Jim, and me standing at the end of the driveway in 2005.*

Top: *Gary, me, Bruce, Maxine, Bob, and June in 1996.*
Bottom: *The Latimer family*

Printed in the United States
By Bookmasters